WELCOME
HOME

Interior design by Amy Ray

WELCOME
HOME

by Brett Hollis

In Dedication
To the memory of Alice "Grandma" Gaenz
A Woman of Prayer

Contents

Preface

What you're about to read is a glimpse into a time of my life that was very difficult for me. But the struggles I lived through do not compare to the triumphs that followed. I am no stranger to emotional pain and distress. And I'm more familiar with depression than anyone would ever want to be. I know these well. What I know even better is freedom from their chains and ruthless torment.

I know I am not the only one who has suffered under difficult circumstances. In fact, comparatively, my trials might seem like nothing to many readers. No doubt some of you have had to overcome obstacles in life to which I cannot relate, or possibly even imagine.

Whether you can relate to me or not, my purpose in writing this is to encourage you by knowing that even in the darkest of times there is a light of hope. That light of hope, you will see, is God's grace and love expressed through His Son. He truly is larger than life and I wish to highlight that throughout these pages. If it wasn't for Him I wouldn't be here to write this.

You matter! You matter to those around you. You matter to me. But most of all, you matter to God. If you question what I just said, trust me, I didn't always believe it either. Here's how I came to know this to be true…

CHAPTER ONE
My Background

"When you are 18 and move out of this house you can do whatever you want. But until then you will do what I say!" Growing up, this was one of the most common phrases I heard come out of my mom's mouth. She wouldn't just blurt it out for any reason at all. It was a statement lying on a spring-loaded tongue that released during an argument or complaint I had about doing or not doing something that she wanted me to do. Not only did it get her point across to me and end all arguments, but it gave me hope for the future and made me really look forward to that day when I no longer had to listen to her and do what she said. I couldn't wait to be 18. That birthday couldn't come fast enough.

As it turned out it did come fast enough; perhaps in some ways, it came too quickly. Turning 18, graduating from high school and moving out of the house, ended up not turning out exactly how I had expected. Ironically, after moving out, the two words I most wanted to hear were, "Welcome Home."

My upbringing was great in most respects. Born into a fun-loving, God-fearing family, I was sandwiched in by church going Christians on both sides – Hollises (Dad's side) & Gaenzes (Mom's side). Growing up with Christian grandparents, aunts, uncles, and cousins was very beneficial to me even if I didn't realize it at the time. When you climb down the family tree and get closer to our roots it is easy to see we had quite a Godly heritage. My Grandpa Hollis had five brothers and every one of them was a preacher ordained through the Assemblies of God Church. My Grandpa and Grandma Gaenz were devoted followers of Jesus and participated in church meetings every time the doors were open. They also traveled, serving in short term mission trips helping spread God's Word. However, having parents that were committed Christians proved to be more influential than anything else. Growing up I assumed my parents had just been born Christian. Before going any further I should probably explain what I mean by "Christian."

A Christian is one who believes with all their heart that Jesus is the Son of God and that He paid the price for their sins by dying on a cross. A Christian believes that this same Jesus who died on the cross rose from the dead three days later overcoming death and proving to all He truly is God's Son sent into the world not to condemn it but to save it. Therefore, a Christian is one who accepts Jesus as his or her personal Lord and Savior and chooses to follow Him, walking in His ways with the help of the Holy Spirit who lives in them. It is this belief and this tradition I was born into.

Both sides of my family were Christians and yet both sides, like any family, had their issues too. However, I must say that my dad, in my eyes, seemed like a perfect angel. I always assumed Dad came out of Grandma's womb as a born again believer primed for his first gold star in Sunday school. I say this because he was always so good. He was an usher at church and a deacon for many years. Dad is 64 years old now and to this day remains one of the greatest examples of Godly character to me and my family. My mom never came across quite as innocent as my dad. However, she was devoted to daily study of the Bible, to daily prayer, and to playing the piano in church every Sunday morning. Mom and Dad would say prayers with me as they tucked me in at night. Once I started school Mom read the Bible to me every day as I ate breakfast. There were many days I was not interested in her reading the Bible. It was sometimes annoying, especially since I was not a morning person, but looking back now I am so grateful for her insistence on this morning family ritual.

I grew up believing God not only existed but that He was with me at all times. Between my family upbringing and the teaching I received at church, having Jesus "in my heart" was a part of my basic understanding of what I needed in life. I do not remember a specific time as a child when I may have asked Jesus into my heart, but I don't ever remember a time when I didn't feel He was there. Well, that is until I was 18, and that is where this story really begins.

We faithfully attended church every Sunday morning and evening with Sunday school squeezed in between. I enjoyed the church because I had many friends there, but the services, singing, and classes I could do without. There was no meaning behind it, unless I happened to give the right answer in class before anyone else and win my choice of a Tootsie Roll or hard candy. But that unfortunately didn't happen too often.

My spiritual journey is an interesting one. Parts of it I still don't understand to this day; but, I will try to relate it to the best of my ability.

Throughout my life, like all of us, I have been in a war zone; the battle between good and evil. I was very attracted to the rebellious side of things. Much of this goes back to my desire to be like my uncle

Wayne. Uncle Wayne (my mom's youngest brother), unlike the rest of the family, was not a professing, church attending Christian. He often spoke of himself as the "Black Sheep" of the family. He smoked, swore, looked at Playboy, didn't go to church, didn't pray at meal time, told dirty jokes, talked tough, and carried himself with confidence. A man of short stature (about 5'8") his presence somehow seemed to demand respect. He was just all around cool. I wanted that. I wanted significance. I wanted to be known for something. I wanted to be him.

By my senior year of high school not only had I lost my virginity but I felt like I was losing hope and even my sense of self. Who was I? I was smoking a pack of cigarettes a day, swearing like a drunken sailor and always trying to find new ways to rebel against my parents and everything I had been taught growing up. In all of this I still had love and respect for my family members, church members, and most people around me; but, there was something in me that wanted to be a rebel. It's almost like I wanted a name for myself. Within me was this strange desire to want to worry my parents. It's like I wanted them to worry about me and whether or not I would make it to heaven or even make it home at night. Sad as it is, that was my attitude. The tension rose between me and my folks during my senior year. It wasn't their fault. It was mine. I take all the blame. They were great parents doing the best they knew how. Having me as a kid would have pushed an atheist parent to pray. The more I rebelled, the more my parents came down on me. We were just not getting along.

It was during my senior year of high school I began to really struggle emotionally. No one at school knew I was struggling because I would do my best to cover my real feelings with humor. The funny thing (pun intended) is I was making others laugh and smile while I was finding it almost impossible to find anything good or positive in my own life. Depression began to set in my mind like the sun setting in the west. Everything was becoming darker by the minute. When asked now what was wrong then, it is always a difficult question for me to answer. Looking back I am convinced my empty feelings were the result of years of running from God. I wanted to rebel. I wanted to be the Black Sheep of our family. There was an image I was looking for. As someone once said, I had a God shaped hole in my heart and He was the only one that could fill it; but I kept trying to fill that hole with everything else I could think of. Trying to ignore hopeless thoughts and feelings all day long can take a toll on you. All my energy was zapped and I was left feeling like all the wind had been knocked out of me. The nasty part of depression is that when you are depressed you often don't know why. Then it becomes a vicious cycle. You fall further into despair because you don't know why you are so sad and this makes you feel even worse because you know there is no logical reason for you to feel the way you do.

I didn't want to tell anyone. Depression was my secret. Why did I keep it a secret? Good question. After all, there were plenty of caring people in my life who would have gone out of their way to help me. My Aunt Beth lovingly listened to me as I shared with her some of my struggles, but even then

I refrained from telling her everything. Although she encouraged me, I still kept her at bay when it came to my deepest of feelings. Looking back now, I realize how selfish, inconsiderate, and foolish I was by not reaching out for help. There are so many people in the world today who have no one close to them that they feel safe in sharing things with. Many come from broken homes lacking support of any kind. And here I was, surrounded by a large, incredible family, lots of caring people at church and even teachers at school and never once did I reach out to anyone. There were a few reasons I didn't reach out. One, I think, was pride. I didn't want to seem weak and look like I couldn't handle life. Two, I don't think I wanted all the attention. What I mean is I didn't want everyone to know about how I was feeling and want everyone praying for me and asking me questions. Three, I was depressed. And when you are depressed you are driven by emotions not logic. Plus when you are depressed you often don't know why you're depressed so what is there to talk about? What needs to be fixed? These may not seem like good reasons to have hidden my pain from others but then again I wasn't very reasonable at that stage in my life. It is what it was.

CHAPTER TWO
Erin

I n early summer, shortly after graduation, I began dating a girl named Erin. I really liked Erin and even though I was struggling in a number of ways, I did enjoy portions of that summer including time spent with my new girlfriend.

As fall began to set in, many friends from High School were going off to college and it was beginning to hit me that I had now graduated and needed to decide what I was going to do with my life. By this time I began to work basically full time for my parents helping them build their new house in Kent, Washington. Carpentry was something my grandfather passed down to my dad and uncles, but it made a huge leap over me and my generation. I hated it. The only part of working on the house that I really enjoyed was cutting and splitting the firewood while clearing the lot. I think this added to my frustration because I was already walking around with a cloud over me. I knew I needed to find some sort of career but this definitely wasn't it. However, it was the only thing I could do at the time. I lived in a motorhome on my parents property in order to help keep watch over the tools and construction equipment and also to get out of the house. My parents and I were not getting along so well by this point and it was good to just get away. I still had my room back at the duplex my parents were renting, but the motorhome was where I spent most of my time. The motorhome belonged to my uncle Wayne and he was letting us borrow it. It was an early 60's Cortez model and was so ugly he nicknamed it Motor-homely. I lived there with Larry, my cat, watching over the property and enjoying a little freedom each night.

It was an early November evening when Erin came to the motorhome to see me. During the course of our short visit she told me she wanted to break up. When she said those words I could feel this stirring of emotions in me. I was crushed. There was a new hollowness inside me. However, being a guy I didn't want her to think I was weak in any way so she never got to see these emotions surface. She got into her car and drove away leaving me wondering if I would ever see her again. I remember running in the dark through the woods, the bushes beating against my legs, to get one last glimpse of Erin as she drove down 272nd street behind the property. She couldn't see me as she passed by but I watched intently until I could no longer see her tail lights. Gently twirling the top of the tall grass blades with my hand I stood there still staring at the dark empty highway, realizing that what I was seeing was really just a glimpse of my heart and future – dark and empty and alone. When I could no longer hear the sound of her car I made the lonely descent back to the motorhome.

The sadness that came over me was so real and painful, like a knife in my chest. I was dumbfounded with almost frantic thoughts about what to do next. That night I lay in my small bed feeling lonelier than ever. Staring at the ceiling partially lit by the moon peeking through the drapes, I found myself going back to my roots and praying to God, asking Him to take this pain away and make me happy. Faith rose up in me believing that when I woke up in the morning I would be alright and these sad feelings would be gone. Instead, what little faith I had died overnight like a flower planted in shallow soil. The flower of faith had been choked out by the weeds of pain and depression. My prayers were not answered.

I woke up still hurting, still confused. When I realized this was not just a bad dream and was indeed a reality, and that God obviously didn't care about my pain and what I was going through, I sat there quietly and lit a cigarette. I started that day driven by the hurt that was now full grown in me. My view of life was becoming obstructed by the weeds of emotions that were quickly growing into a dark forest within.

CHAPTER THREE

Preparing For My
Hunting Trip

T he only thing that gave me a glimmer of happiness was that I was going to be leaving in a couple days to go elk hunting with my uncle Dan (my dad's younger brother). Dan was a really cool guy. He was a tall (6'6"), thin man who loved to hunt and have a good time. He always made me laugh and he seemed to be different in some ways from his brothers and sisters. He knew Jesus, but the path he followed didn't seem as narrow and straight as the rest of his family. This obviously was appealing to me.

Something happened (I don't remember what) the day I was packing for my hunting trip that triggered some arguments between my parents and I making me want to head to the mountains even more. The night before I was to leave I went over to Jeff's place. Jeff Hagan was my best friend. We had so much in common and loved to hang out together. We told each other everything and yet I still didn't even tell Jeff the depth of how I was feeling. He knew I was discouraged because Erin broke up with me. He also knew I wasn't getting along with my parents but I never told him I was feeling depressed or about my prayer the night before. We stood outside in his driveway smoking cigarettes and talking about life. After a few cigarettes I turned to Jeff and said, "Two things I will never do. I will never quit smoking and I will never go back to church again." The thoughts behind these words I believe were to somehow hurt God the way I felt He was hurting me. My emotional pain was beginning to turn into anger toward God. I was trying to find a way to get back at Him for giving me such a horrible life. I felt betrayed. Flicking the smoldering butt of my last cigarette onto the quiet street, I got into my truck and drove back to the motorhome for another lonely night by myself.

Waking to the alarm clock I tried feeling better

by reminding myself that I was heading to the mountains that day to go hunting. That should cure all. I loaded my things into the old truck and I headed to Uncle Dan's house. When I arrived he wasn't quite ready to go, so we just visited while he gathered all of his gear together. Finally his Blazer was packed and we headed to Yakima. Being with Uncle Dan was always fun, so on the drive; I was having moments of actually feeling better. But once the laughter died down and I had time to just stare out my window with music playing on his stereo I would be reminded of Erin in some way and the misery would set back in.

CHAPTER FOUR
The Motel

Arriving in the city of Yakima, east of the mountains, early that evening we checked into our motel and began to unload our belongings into our second-story room. Once the Blazer was unloaded we decided to go to a local restaurant and get a bite to eat before it got too late. After dinner we went back to the motel where we hung out and talked hunting and anything else that came to mind.

Not wanting Uncle Dan to know anything was wrong with me and wanting to keep my pride in tact I never shared with him how tormented I was feeling inside. It is hard to explain the pain I was going through but it began to manifest itself in strange ways. I was smoking cigarettes quite a bit back then, but on this particular trip I craved them more than anything. Each drag of a cigarette somehow seemed to dull the pain a little.

As Uncle Dan was in the motel getting situated for the night I, with my cigarette, stood out on the second story walkway overlooking the parking lot. While standing out there I began to feel an enormous rage surging through me. Anger was boiling up in me and like the lava in a volcano it was getting ready to erupt and was looking for a target to spew itself toward. I saw a stranger below in the parking lot. Something rose up inside of me that wanted to pick a fight with him. I kept staring at him hoping he would give me a reason to come down and fight. Whether it was a crooked look, a cocky comment, or even a small glance, I wanted to fight.

This was a bit strange for me, to say the least. First of all, I always wanted to be everyone's friend growing up. I enjoyed being friends with all the different groups or "cliques" in school and made it a habit to try and make people laugh. As a boy I always had an interest in fighting but nothing out of the ordinary. In fact, whenever I was someplace where a fight was about to take place or if someone wanted to fight me I always got butterflies in my stomach and would get really nervous. Plus, I was not known for my fighting skills. Not that I couldn't hold my own or at least go down trying – it just wasn't a part of my reputation. But something changed. After graduation the more depressed I became the more I was drawn toward violence and a desire to fight. This night it was really stirring in me.

As this guy strolled by I kept taking quick drags of my cigarette and pacing back and forth hoping something would instigate a brawl. He kept walking without even noticing me and I kept pacing, watching him until he was out of sight. I never said anything to him and he never even looked at me. But the anger was there. Taking the last drag of my smoke I flicked the burning butt off the balcony and headed back into the motel room.

I retired to bed for the night and watched some TV before shutting off the lights. The laughter I experienced while watching TV and visiting with Uncle Dan was real for me. There was nothing fake about it. The show ended, the lights went out and the laughter stopped for another night. Depression just has a way of coming on strong when it's quiet and there is nothing distracting you but your own thoughts and feelings, like lying in bed with the lights off. The darkness of the room was no match to the darkness I felt in my heart. I was with one of my best friends and yet I was so lonely. I was safe in a motel room, yet I felt so scared. My life was filled with love from others, yet anger and hatred were overtaking me. And then I fell asleep.

CHAPTER FIVE
Day One of Hunting

The next morning I actually woke up feeling pretty good. Uncle Dan was happy and being his goofy self getting ready and the idea of maybe bagging my first elk was really appealing to me. It was dark out with a nice November chill in the air. After loading up the Blazer we headed toward the hills. It was about a half-hour drive to where we were going. We headed down highway 410 west toward Bald Mountain where we decided to hunt for the day.

Bald Mountain and the surrounding areas were known for their large elk herds. Uncle Dan had hunted this area quite a few times in the past but it was still fairly new territory for me. I had been over there a couple times with him before, but we mainly hunted Bethel Ridge on the other side of the highway and some other nearby spots. As we turned off the highway and headed up the mountainside, my attention was jumping around from things Uncle Dan would say to the terrain out my window, from hoping to see an elk back to how sad and mad I was feeling. We spent the whole day up on this mountain.

Sometimes we hiked together but most of the time we would split up for a few hours and then meet back up with each other. Walking through the woods I just began to feel worse and worse. Hunting wasn't even appealing to me and that in itself scared me. After hiking for a while I would find a log or rock to sit on and then I would just stare off into the distance without paying attention to what was going on around me. I wasn't looking for elk; I was looking for peace and happiness. There was a blizzard of turmoil in me and I found I was talking a lot to myself and God. I was becoming very angry with God and I voiced it to Him while I hunted that weekend. The first day of hunting was over and Uncle Dan and I were sitting back at our motel. Uncle Dan was being funny and goofy and I was trying to act like I was having a good time.

CHAPTER SIX
Day Two of Hunting

The next morning came soon enough and we went through the same routine that we had the day before. It was November 12, 1989. We drove once again to Bald Mountain just outside Yakima. Driving up the same forest road we had been hunting before, we parked about half way up the mountain on the side of the road. Then we made our game plan for the day. Uncle Dan voiced his desire to hunt a particular area, and I said I would cover another area in the opposite direction. Loading our guns and gear we agreed to meet back at the Blazer in three hours and Uncle Dan headed off into the woods. Acting like I was still getting my gear together I waited until he was out of sight and I leaned my rifle against a tree and lit up a cigarette.

I was in no hurry to go anywhere. In fact, I really

didn't want to be out hunting. The longer I stood there the more irate I became at God, life, everything. Slinging my rifle over my shoulder I started hiking into the woods. Instead of hiking quietly as I had been taught and which was my normal routine, I just crashed my way through the countryside not caring and making so much noise there was no chance of me seeing an elk. With every step I took, a fierce anger was growing within me. I became overwhelmed with despair and rage. So much so that I felt if I were to look into a mirror my eyes would be red with anger. Not paying attention to where I was going I stopped and lit a cigarette. Immediately after finishing that one I lit another. There I was, just standing there smoking, with my thoughts as cloudy as the smoke billowing from my mouth. As I finished my third cigarette, I dropped it to the ground and rubbed it into the forest floor of dirt and nettles with my boot. Breaking the early morning silence I looked up to the sky and began to yell.

I yelled at God and began to cuss Him out as though it was someone I hated from school. My shouts hushed the birds as my voice echoed through the canyon ricocheting off the trees and landing in their maker's ear. I told God I hated Him. Over and over I said, "I hate you God. You %#! #*&$% @#^&$!!! I hate you!!! Everybody says you're there. My mom and dad say you're there, Pastor Brooks says you're there." And then out of desperation, with anguish mixed with surrender, I said, "If you're there then take me home because I'm lost! Take me home!"

At this point I took the .300 H&H Magnum I had slung over my shoulder and I looked at it in fear and hesitation. Shaking, with my emotions out of control, I took my rifle and pressed the end of the cold barrel beneath my chin. Deep down I knew this was not what I wanted to do, and I was scared that I even had this thought. I took the safety off and slowly moved my finger toward the trigger. Finding the trigger, my finger stayed for only a split second before I removed it. I removed my finger from the trigger for two reasons. One, I was afraid. But two, I suddenly felt a calming sensation come over me.

One minute I was shaking in fury and the next minute I was as calm as I have ever been. It was a different kind of calm; a calm that came from the outside and over me without my permission. Sensing this tranquility I pulled my finger away and removed the rifle from its position and stood there calmly, the muzzle now pointed at the ground. It was a strange calm. I was confused as to how the moments leading up to this could be so different. First, I was shaking on the inside and shaking on the outside and now nothing. I quickly put the safety on again and stood there for a few moments. I stood there quizzically trying to figure out what was going on. What just happened? What changed? What was different? I didn't know the answers to these questions; but, as I stood there, that calming sensation slowly washed over me like a gentle shower from my head down over the rest of my body.

For some reason my attention was directed to my feet, and as I looked I saw my cigarette butts crinkled in the dirt below. What really caught my attention was a path that started right where I was standing.

When I was yelling at God I was facing in such a way where there was no path. But when I was finished and turned around there was a well-maintained path leading up through the woods beginning where I was standing. Following the path with my eyes I could see that it made its way through the woods in a seemingly straight line. Grabbing hold of the sling and placing my rifle over my shoulder I decided to follow this path not knowing where it was headed.

I was befuddled and curious because this is the same terrain I hunted the day before and I didn't remember ever seeing this path before now. So I began hiking. The path was straight, smooth and level for the first part and then it began to change and become steep and rugged. After trudging my way up this hill I began to get winded and tired as it was getting steeper and rockier in places. Half way up this hill I stopped to take a break. While standing there I looked around while trying to catch my breath. Seeing where I had come from, I was momentarily trying to figure out if the path I was on ended or began right where I had been standing when I cursed God. A few minutes later I was ready to continue following the path. With one more glance down the hill I turned my attention up the steep slope where the path headed.

Getting a second wind in my lungs I continued my journey hoping to make sense of some of my feelings and thoughts as I plodded on. Walking up the hill I was looking off to my right admiring the mountain tops and sneaking peeks through the trees at the valleys below. As I was getting closer to what seemed to be the top, the sun was shining through the branches of the trees with such brilliance that it almost eclipsed the large tree trunks between us. I put my head down as I completed some more steps and at one point when I lifted my head the sun was so bright in my eyes that I said to myself out loud "I wish I would have brought some sun glasses." The closer to the top of the hill I got the brighter the sun was in my eyes. Suddenly it dawned on me…every morning I have hiked this mountain the sun has been coming up to my right. When I turned and looked over to my right the sun was coming up over there. It was just beginning to crest over some mountain peaks. But when I turned back to my left (now facing north and forward again) in the direction I was seeing the sun light I saw something different... better, brighter.

I saw a big open area of fresh green grass and flowers. It was beautiful and pleasant as well as out of the ordinary and strangely placed because it was the middle of November and everything around me was dead – the grass, plants etc. There was a tree stump in the middle of this miniature paradise and standing next to the stump was Jesus Christ.

I knew it was Him; there was no doubt in my mind. I had never experienced anything like this: a vision so real, so amazing and so powerful that for the first time in a long time I instantly forgot about any problems or distraught feelings. I was engulfed by what I saw, tuning out the rest of the world around me. He stood taller than I and He was wearing a shiny bright white robe with a blue silky sash covering His left shoulder draping across His chest and resting on His right hip. He had brown shoulder length hair, a beard and mustache as well. He smiled the most friendly, inviting smile and reaching out His right hand toward me He said, "Welcome home Brett. Welcome home." There was something so significant to me about His mouth. The thought of His lips opening to a smile made an everlasting impression on me. The way He smiled and spoke made every care of mine melt away like wax to a flame. He didn't touch me, nor did He stay in bodily form or have any sort of conversation with me beyond what was already said. The next thing I knew, I found myself sitting on the very stump I had seen Him near surrounded by the green grass.

There was a presence that I find nearly impossible to describe. It was a stopping presence. It seemed to stop time, stop creation and stop the pain I had grown accustom to. Peace came into me like a raging river bringing my emotions to a new flood stage, washing away all the negative feelings that stood in its path. I sat on that stump with my head down and I wept and wept. Crying was significant for me because it had been so long since the last time I had cried – perhaps years. Having developed that tough outer shell it was almost as though I couldn't cry even if I wanted. That was until now. I couldn't stop crying and I didn't want to stop crying. Those tears were like a healing balm that came from deep within me. Streaming down my cheeks and falling off the edge of my jawbone they disappeared into the fabric of my old flannel shirt. I honestly don't know how long I sat on that stump crying. It could of have been 5 minutes; it could have been 5 hours. Time meant nothing to me and yet in a strange way time was beginning to mean everything. I felt so good, so happy and free. Free from pain. Free from worry. Free from anger. And free from myself. As the tears began to slow down and the cool mountain breeze dried them on my face I looked up and noticed six mule deer standing perfectly still staring at me. They showed no signs of fear whatsoever. In fact they were standing next to each other in a line and one by one they walked peacefully almost like they didn't want to disturb me. One at a time they walked gently to my left, behind me and down the hill to my right where I had come from. A big grin covered my face as I thought to myself the one time I didn't feel like killing anything and there were six deer standing right in front of me. Even though I knew it wasn't deer season I always chuckled to myself about that. It was the calm after the storm. I was so sorry and ashamed for yelling at God, accusing Him, calling Him names and such. But as sorry as I was I didn't dwell on it because of the amazing peace that was engulfing me at the time and I knew in my heart I was forgiven. Nothing mattered to me at this point; but, in a different way than just an hour prior. I was okay and none of the problems that haunted me earlier that day seemed to exist any longer. They were gone like a faded memory. Looking down at my watch I discovered I had been sitting on that stump for quite a while, and I was supposed to meet Uncle Dan at the Blazer in about 10 minutes (a little more than the amount of time it would take me to hike back). So I started my trek.

As I hiked toward the Blazer I kept replaying the events I had experienced in my mind. What just happened? Did it really happen or am I just going crazy and making this up? With each step I thought about the details and even began to recite each moment aloud to myself. The closer I got to the Blazer the more concerned I became with what I was supposed to do about this encounter. There was a mixture of elation and questions swishing around in my mind. Why did this happen to me? What is going on? My biggest worry at the moment was trying to decide what to tell Uncle Dan or if I should tell him anything at all. Do I keep this a secret? Do I tell him? If I tell him, will he think I'm nuts or that I had lost it? Will he not trust me anymore with a gun or go hunting with me? Am I losing it? All of these thoughts and questions energized me as I briskly moved through the woods back to the Blazer.

Having taken a different route back I found myself ducking to get through many thick bushes to find my way, but not bothered or distracted by the extra work as my mind was so focused. With one hand holding my rifle down to keep it from getting scratched, the other hand was lifting prickly branches over my head to get through small openings in the bushes. I pushed my way through and came out right near the Blazer.

I could see Uncle Dan there unloading his rifle and putting his gear away. Taking a deep breath I climbed the small incline leading up to where the Blazer was parked. As I approached Uncle Dan he turned and so naturally said, "Did you see anything?" Although this is a very common question we ask each other after hunting apart, this time it was different. His question hit me harder than any time before. I wasn't sure how to answer. But in order to not make it seem awkward I just said "No. Not really, just a few deer." With a smile forming on my face I turned and looked into the woods and unloaded my gun. I held onto a secret hope of seeing Jesus again.

It was as though His presence followed me out of the woods and I knew He was there but this time out of sight. Part of me really wanted to tell Uncle Dan but for some reason I held it all in. We got back to the motel, had dinner, and were getting ready for bed when our telephone rang. It was my mom.

Something was wrong. She sounded like she had been crying and she told me she had bad news. A longtime friend of the family, Jack Erickson, had passed away. I really liked Jack and always enjoyed when we would go to his home in Sequim, WA, to visit. He and his wife, Marie, had a really neat house, not too far from the beach, and a chicken coop full of chickens. My brother, Brandon, and I would get fresh eggs from the coop for breakfast whenever we spent the night. We thought that was so cool. But when Mom told me about Jack's death it wasn't so much the fact that Jack died that hit me. It was the coincidence of Jack dying the same week I came so close to taking my own life and listening to how sad my mom was. After hanging up the phone I went out on our balcony to have a cigarette.

A knot formed in my stomach. It dawned on me how badly I would have hurt my mom had God not intervened. Finishing my cigarette, I walked back into our room and headed straight for the bathroom. Locking the door behind me I stood in front of the sink staring into the mirror. I moved closer to the mirror and just stared into my eyes. My pupils seemed to go on forever. Who was I to cheat death?

Did today really happen? Why am I here? How could I have done this to my mom and dad? God, I don't understand. A circle of fog was developing near my mouth as I asked these questions out loud with my face nearly touching the mirror. My questions were not answered and I retired to bed for the evening. We had one more day of hunting and then we were heading home.

CHAPTER SEVEN
The Day After

Waking up the next morning it didn't take me long to get out of bed – and that is saying a lot because I was not a morning person. I couldn't wait to get back out in the woods. I wanted to get back to that same spot and see if I could make sense of the previous day's experience. Excited yet cautious, I headed down the road. Uncle Dan still had no idea what I had experienced the day before and I wanted it that way for the time being. We pulled off the main highway and started heading up the same forest service road we had been hunting off of all weekend. Uncle Dan asked me if I had a preference of where I wanted to hunt that morning. Without hesitation I told him I wanted to go back to the same spot I was hunting the day before because I felt there was potential of finding something there. Parking the Blazer in the same spot we got out, loaded our rifles and agreed once again to meet back in three hours. It didn't take me long at all to head off into the woods.

I was so full of anticipation. Just the idea of being with Jesus again was more than thrilling to me. Navigating my way through the woods I tried to follow the same path as the day before. I was walking fast, making noise and once again not caring if I saw an elk. But this time I was running to Jesus, not from Him. Finally I found the spot where I had yelled at God and had carelessly mishandled my rifle, testing God with my life. Cigarette butts lay crinkled in the dirt surrounded by my boot-prints. But there was no path. I looked in both directions and the path I had followed the day before was not there.

Standing there in silence, I remembered the awful things I had said to God in this very spot nearly 24 hours earlier. It sent chills of shame down my spine that I had treated Him like that. But before those memories had a chance to spoil my day they were washed away with the thoughts of how Jesus intervened and saved my life, even after the way I had treated Him. He responded to my hate with His love. His love won. My pace was much faster this time as I continued my search through the woods. Without having the path as my guide I began hiking in the direction I remembered going the day before. Reaching the steepest part of the hill a smile was permanently pressed on my face when I looked east at the sun cresting over the mountain tops. No bright and shiny light in front of me this time. When I reached the top of the hill and looked with anticipation there was no garden-like setting, no green grass or flowers and most disappointing – there was no Jesus. But the stump was still there. Even though there was no vision of Jesus this time, His presence was somehow just as real.

I slowly approached the stump and once again became a bit overwhelmed with emotion. The fact that there was no green grass and flowers or Jesus waiting at the stump didn't seem to faze me. It was obvious – I had experienced a very powerful vision from the Lord. There was such a peace on top of that mountain. With every noise common in the woods such as a squirrel running from tree to tree or leaves falling from the tops of the trees I would look to see if it was Jesus. Even without seeing Him, hope was rising up inside me with joy running parallel to it. Standing in one spot and turning, I kept looking around taking in every detail. A white cold flake hit my hat and melted on impact. Another one landed on my sleeve. It was beginning to snow. It didn't take long for the speed and amount of snow to increase. I decided I better get going so as not to get lost. There was no telling what kind of storm was heading our way. The snow was coming down pretty hard but it seemed as though I was finding my way easily as the trees held most of the snow off the path. The entire time I hiked I talked with Jesus.

I couldn't see Him but He felt so near me, just like the day before. It was the best walk I had ever had. I talked and talked knowing I had someone listening to me, not just someone – the Lord and my new best friend. Thinking about it later made me laugh because I wondered what another hunter would have thought if he saw me walking through the woods talking to my "friend." He probably would have called the authorities on me.

Finding an old logging road at the top of this particular area, I began to walk in the direction of the Blazer. While walking the road I asked the Lord, out loud as I had been all morning, why He did this. I said, "Why me? Why did you save me?" Just as clearly as I have ever heard a voice, He spoke to me. It wasn't audible, but it was so strong and clear within my spirit that I knew exactly what He was saying.

He said, "Look down the road you just came from." So I did. I had been walking on this old logging road. The trees had grown close together toward their tops which made a natural canopy keeping the snow from landing on the road. Instead it was resting on all the branches and then some of it was turning to big drops of cold water falling through the pine needles making the road below muddy. The trees were adding a dark shade making the road look gloomy and dreary. Then the Lord continued saying, "That's your life. That's your last 18 years. You can continue walking this way but that is all you will have to show for it. Or you can start walking with me and this is what I will give you." At that moment I knew I was to turn back to my right in the direction I had been walking. When I did I noticed the tree line over the road ended where I was standing and the road continued up through the mountains covered with fresh virgin snow. It was a pure white road. There were no vehicle tracks or even animal tracks on it, just pure white for as far as my eyes could see. His voice was silent to the human ear but loud in the core of my being and I responded out loud, "Let's walk, let's talk and let's not stop."

Having grown up in the church and listening to my Sunday school teachers, I felt it would only make this proper and seal the deal for me to officially invite Jesus into my heart and ask Him to forgive me of all my sins saving my soul from sin and death. So that's exactly what I did. Not being a master of words or really knowing exactly what I should say or how to say it, I just said, "Jesus, please forgive me for all my sins and come into my heart and save me." And that was that. With a grin covering the width of my face

I headed down my new path, the road of pure white snow, leaving behind the dark muddy road forever. My talking didn't miss a beat as I walked that road back to the Blazer full of true joy. One thing I said to the Lord out there was that I wanted Him to use me to help others like me. Little did I know how the answer to that simple request would end up looking. I made it back to the Blazer and we put away our equipment one last time. We were heading home. Our hunting trip was over for another year but my new life was just getting started.

CHAPTER EIGHT
The Drive Home

As we headed down the snowy forest road, I popped in a Phil Collins tape and played his song Take Me Home. As I listened to this song I couldn't help smiling as I looked out my window watching the trees pass by. I felt like I was now home – spiritually speaking. But as we changed from the service road to Highway 410 and headed over Chinook Pass, I was still confused why God saved me and why I was still alive and suddenly my thoughts shifted to thinking I was probably going to die on the way home.

Here's how I came to this conclusion. God knew I was going to die on the way home but I wasn't ready. So He allowed me to have that experience to prepare me for death. That may seem strange to you reading this, but for me at the time it was the only conclusion

I could come up with that made sense. Apparently I had forgotten or disregarded my prayer for God to use me to help others because I was convinced I was going to die on the way home. With every passing car I thought we were going to be in an accident which would result in my death. After about three hours of driving and thinking I was going to die we pulled into Uncle Dan's driveway in Auburn accident free. Of course, I thought, we weren't going to get in a wreck while together. It wasn't going to be Uncle Dan's time to go. Now I was convinced I was going to die while driving my truck home from Uncle Dan's. Fifteen minutes later, to my surprise, I pulled my truck up to our duplex as safe as when I first left. I turned the truck off and sat there for a couple minutes trying to wrap my head around the past few days and figure out what I was going to do now that I was home, safe and alive. I made it. Now what?

CHAPTER NINE
Back Home

I thought, I can't tell Mom and Dad what happened. If I tell them they will either think I'm crazy or they will get all mushy on me and want to make a big deal out of it to everyone. I didn't want that kind of attention. Pride was still strong inside me. My last interaction with them before leaving was an argument and things had not been too good between us leading up to my hunting trip. That's it, I decided: I will follow Jesus, but secretly, without letting my parents know what happened. I don't know why this was my decision but, as I said, pride still had some big chains on me and I just didn't want them to know everything. Stepping out of my truck I grabbed my rifle cases and headed across the street to the duplex. Setting the cases down to open the front door I took one last deep breath before turning the knob and entering. Pushing the door open, I grabbed the cases and worked my way in making no small commotion with the cases banging into the door to keep it open as the screen door was bumping the back of me.

Dad and Mom were sitting directly ahead in the living room watching TV. They said hi and I burst into tears like a baby who just lost his favorite toy. In a tear-filled cracked voice I said, "Mom I need to talk to you," and leaving my gun cases in the entry I hurried up to my bedroom and sat on my bed waiting for her to get there. I knew it wouldn't take her long and the thought of not telling my parents was obviously a forgotten idea now hidden in the reality of the moment. I sat on my bed trembling but not with fear. My tremors were more induced by joy, this new life I was feeling in me and remorse over my sin and how I had treated my parents.

Speaking of my parents, I don't know why I didn't ask my dad to come up or why I didn't just sit down in the living room with them and share what happened with both of them. This has bothered me ever since. I don't think it was fair to my dad and I'm sure it hurt his feelings. I know if it was me, and my son did the same thing, there would be a sense of pain in my heart. Even now, I am full of regret when I reflect on those moments. If I could do it all over I would have told them both that night. Pride may have had something to do with it. But I think primarily it was because I usually felt more comfortable talking to my mom about issues in life. I always knew Dad cared and even deserved to know things but he didn't pursue those kinds of talks with me like Mom did. Whatever the reason, it was only Mom who I invited into my room that night.

She came running up the stairs and walked through the partially open door. There I was sitting on the bed with tears streaming down my face. Mom's face contorted to a worried look as she closed my door and sat next to me with her left hand rubbing my back and her right hand rubbing my forearm. The moment she saw me crying she knew I had had an encounter with the Lord; however, worry was overtaking her countenance as she continued rubbing my back and asking in her soft mom voice, "What is it babe?

What's wrong? What happened?"

The words just weren't coming out. Every time I tried to say something my sobbing got in the way. Finally I calmed down enough to share what happened to me on that mountain. As I gave her an account of my weekend I could tell that she was having mixed feelings. Now tears were beginning to flow down her cheeks and the abrupt knowledge that her "baby boy" almost took his own life was driving a sword of emotional pain right through her heart but it was walking a balance beam of unexpected answers to her prayers for my deliverance and salvation. We were like two washing machines at a laundromat sitting next to each other both on spin cycles, both with a load of emotions tumbling into each other. Knowing there would be plenty of time to sort through our emotional laundry later; we both sat there and cried while she held onto me tightly with the gentleness of a mothers love. But, it was a nervous hold that was afraid to let go. When the faucets of our eyes seemed to slow down Mom looked at me and let me know how glad she was that I did not go through with killing myself and how she had spent so many hours, days and years praying for me. My one request to her was that she tell no one except my dad. I really wanted my dad to know but for some reason I wanted her to have the task of telling him. If anyone else was to know, I wanted it to come from me and not her. Knowing my mom is a woman of her word I knew she would respect my wishes. We hugged, she went downstairs and I went to bed.

As I lay in bed that night I stared at the ceiling and thought back through everything that had happened during the weekend. Questions filled my mind of what life was going to be like from now on. How was it all going to change? I had a certain reputation among my friends and family and I didn't know what that was going to look like anymore. But my desire to follow Jesus was overriding everything else at this point. My conversations with Jesus were so personal. While lying there I just talked with Him until I fell asleep. It felt good to be home – in more ways than one.

CHAPTER TEN
Grandma Gaenz

Opening my eyes the next morning I started the day by saying "Good morning Jesus." I got up and threw on some pants and a shirt and headed downstairs for some breakfast. Dad had already left for work and Mom was in her room getting ready for the day. As was my normal routine I grabbed the largest bowl in the cupboard and then poured the cereal to the rim. I opened the refrigerator and reached for the milk when the phone rang.

I picked up the receiver and rested it between my head and shoulder so I could talk and pour my milk at the same time. It was Grandma Gaenz. She said, "Hi honey, this is Grandma." I said, "hi Grandma." No sooner did I finish saying hi than she went on to say something I never expected. She said, "Honey, I want you to tell me what happened this weekend.

God had me up all weekend praying for you. I hardly got any sleep. He told me He was going to do something very powerful in your life. Now you tell me what He did for you."

I almost collapsed. I was speechless; I could not believe what I heard her say. Grandma was always a prayer warrior, I knew that. But, I had no idea she had a connection like this. If it wasn't for feeling the chills going up my spine and the goose bumps raising the hair on my arms I would have sworn I was paralyzed by what she said. Tears began to well up in my eyes. Having my cereal turn soggy no longer seemed to matter. I shared with Grandma what had happened over the weekend. When I got to the part about my encounter with Jesus, she broke into reverent laughter mixed with "Praise the Lord" and "Thank you Jesus." When I finished she reassured me that she knew God was going to do something life changing in me while I was in the mountains hunting because God had kept her up all weekend praying and speaking to her about me. I always loved my Grandma Gaenz; but, I never felt closer to her than I did during that phone call. For the rest of her life we had a special connection, different than before. It all stemmed from us having separate experiences that crossed each other's paths that one November day.

Words cannot describe how significant that phone call was to me and has been throughout the years. God used that call to show me that He was in this the whole time and had a plan even when I didn't realize it. The call also helped me in those times when questions or doubts would try to enter my mind regarding my experience. Hanging up the phone, I left my cereal and went upstairs.

I knocked on my mother's bedroom door, and she told me I could come in. I asked her if she had told Grandma Gaenz anything about my experience and she assured me she hadn't. I told her about the phone call I had just received from Grandma and neither of us had much to say because I think we were both so stunned by what was happening. All of this was so exciting to me. I said I needed to go tell Jeff and I took off toward his place.

CHAPTER ELEVEN
Jeff

Jeff lived in a duplex just a few blocks from ours so it didn't take me long to get there. His roommate was gone to work and I knew Jeff was still sleeping so I pounded hard on the door to wake him up. Finally he opened the door and he looked really tired and a bit annoyed that I had woken him – after all he knew that I knew he worked the grave-yard shift. I told him I was sorry for waking him but I had to tell him something that happened to me. We went up to his room and I began to share what God did for me.

His eyes became a shade of red as tears began to develop. I could sense the presence of God as I explained every detail to him. I told Jeff how I had prayed and asked Jesus to forgive me and take over my life and how great I had felt ever since. Jeff wanted to do the same. Before I left, the two of us prayed together and he recommitted his life back to Christ. It was a powerful moment for us both.

Leaving his place I had a peculiar, new excitement in me. Things were happening so fast. It seemed like every time I turned around I was witnessing God doing something powerful. Jeff called me later to tell me that after I left he decided to take a shower and while he was in the shower he was praying and as the water was washing over him he felt this anointed feeling come over him as though the shower was symbolic of God washing all of his sin away. Needless to say he was excited and beginning to change right alongside me.

CHAPTER TWELVE
Pastor Ron Brooks

W hen I got home from Jeff's I had this desire to tell Pastor Brooks. He had been my pastor and a close family friend for most of my life. I knew he would be happy to hear what God had recently done for me. Plus, I thought maybe he could help me figure out this new life and give me some direction. He was no longer the Senior Pastor of Church By the Side of the Road (CBSR), the church I grew up in; but, he was still on their staff as the Missions Pastor. Mom got the church number for me and I called to see if he had any time we could meet and talk. He was happy to hear from me and told me to come on up. I pulled up to the church, parked my truck and walked in. His secretary let him know I was there, and a couple minutes later he came walking out to greet me.

Pastor Brooks greeted me with a smile and hug and said "Why don't we go somewhere and grab a Coke." That sounded good to me. So we walked out to the parking lot and got into his little Honda Prelude. We were hooking our seatbelts and slowly driving through the parking lot toward the entrance to the highway when he stopped the car, turned and looked me in the eye and said, "You had a revelation of Jesus Christ didn't you." The moment he said that the car was filled with the presence of the Holy Spirit and I began to cry – again. I did more crying in the past week than I had during the previous three years. As I wept, Pastor Brooks leaned over and put his arms around me and just held onto me as I cried like a baby in his arms. Once I regained my composure enough to talk, I shared with him what had happened and he gave some resounding "Praise the Lord's" and "Hallelujahs" in return. We went to a restaurant near Sea-Tac Airport and drank a Coke while I filled him in with more details about what was happening in my life. He was so encouraging to me. He seemed genuinely thrilled and made sure I knew he was there for me. Then he said I needed to tell my story.

I needed to let people know what Jesus did for me. And he asked if I would come the following Sunday and share my story at the evening service. He told me to invite my friends and family and he would give me all the time I needed to share that night. I agreed to his invitation. I finished my Coke and we headed back to the church.

Driving home from the church I was trying to think of all the different people I would invite to the service that next Sunday. I was going to need Mom's help getting people there. Uncle Dan and Uncle Wayne were a must. Except, I was a little scared Uncle Wayne would be disappointed in me handling a gun in such a way. And not just any gun – his gun, the one that I had borrowed for the trip. He always taught me to be safe when handling guns. There was also a fear in me that he would think I was weird and not want to spend time with me anymore, not only because I was now "into Jesus," but because I had struggled with depression. He always came across so confident, without any emotional problems, I wasn't sure how this was going to go over. And Uncle Dan – what was

59

I going to say to him? He was the one I was with. He will wonder why I never shared this with him earlier. I was nervous as to how he might respond. I didn't want to hurt him. When I returned home I told Mom and Dad the news that I was going to be sharing my story the next Sunday night and I asked if they would help me invite people. They made several calls to family members and I called my closest friends. We didn't tell anyone the specifics, we just asked if they would come and attend service that following Sunday. Knowing that I, Brett Hollis, was going to be the one sharing must have piqued their curiosity because most everyone we invited showed up.

CHAPTER THIRTEEN
Sharing My Story at CBSR

S unday evening I arrived early and met with
Pastor Brooks. The service began with a time
of singing. Growing up at CBSR I sat through many
worship services, but there was something extra
special about this one. The words to the songs now
had meaning. The choruses that were so familiar
yet previously void of meaning, all of a sudden were
taking me to a place that seemed as close to Jesus as
sitting at his feet. Being a ham for entertainment, I
always loved to be up in front of people. I had been
in just about every Christmas or Easter program the
church had presented since I was five. But tonight
was different. I was nervous; yet, there was a peace.
Like being in a drama waiting for my cue, I sat on
the front pew waiting as Pastor Brooks welcomed
everyone and explained that I was going to be sharing.
As he ended his introduction he extended his arm to

me welcoming me up front. He gave me a hug and handed me the microphone.

Standing up there trying to figure out how I was going to start I looked around and saw so many familiar faces. Faces of people I have known and loved my entire life. Most of my family was sitting off to my right taking up the majority of the section in the back. Uncle Wayne was there. Uncle Dan was there. My brother, parents, cousins, aunts and a number of my other uncles were sitting clumped together on the pews patiently waiting. Then I saw the faces of my old Sunday school teachers, church deacons, and youth leaders. I saw friends I had grown up with in the church and many who I had rebelled with. Everyone sat waiting to hear what I had to say. I could see the curiosity on most of the faces as I held the microphone and prepared to introduce them to the new me. And I began.

They heard how depressed I had been and how badly I wanted to be happy. I told them how I cussed out God and how my rifle almost became an instrument used to end my life. You could have heard a pin drop on the carpeted floor as it struck them and they realized they could have been gathered here for my funeral instead. When I got to the part of me seeing Jesus, I broke down and cried while trying to tell it. Tears flowed down my cheeks as I was reminded of that incredible moment. But it was more than that.

The moment I got to that part of my story I sensed such an overwhelming power come over me as I continued to speak. This power was moving through me and it felt like it was flowing right out of my mouth as I spoke. Most joined in crying right along with me as I finished telling my life-changing story. There was a presence in that sanctuary that was similar to the presence I felt in the woods, in Jeff's room and in Pastor Brooks' Honda. It was the presence of the Holy Spirit – a presence I would soon become very familiar with. Finishing my time of sharing I handed the microphone back to Pastor Brooks who so eloquently brought the service to a close.

With a soft chorus being played in the background

Pastor Brooks shared how this new life I was experiencing is one that God was offering to everyone in the room. That whoever would put their faith in Jesus Christ as their Lord and Savior would also experience this new life being offered. He invited anyone who would like to receive Jesus Christ either for the first time or to rededicate their life to Him to come out of their seats and make their way forward to the front of the church. One by one people came forward. A total of seven people came to know Jesus personally that night and all but one of them were my close friends.

The feelings that were coming over me were amazing. I remember one friend crying almost uncontrollably as Pastor Brooks led them all in a prayer. As the congregation closed the service by singing a song together; Pastor Brooks took us all behind the platform to the church library to talk with us some more. My friend was still weeping as God was pouring His love out on him. Pastor Brooks shared with all of us how important it is going to be to attend a church, read our Bibles and pray. In addition to that he told us how important it would be for us to share this new life experience with others. This I took to heart. After sharing a few more encouraging words he led us all in one last prayer. We all slowly made our way out of the church that night giving hugs and visiting with one another in the foyer. There was no turning back. I was a new person.

The new Brett Hollis had purpose with a whole new set of goals – tell people about Jesus. There was something about my experience of sharing Christ publicly that night that resonated with me. To see so many of my friends come to Christ made me want to see more and more have the same life changing experience. Zeal for God was overtaking me, and I couldn't wait to share it with others.

CHAPTER FOURTEEN
My Story on Tape

Without my knowledge, my story was recorded on audio tape the night I shared it at church. When news of this came, my mom ordered what seemed to be a few crates of these tapes to hand out to friends, family and anyone else who would listen. Before long my story was being heard from coast to coast by people who knew me and some who didn't. This opened up opportunities for me that I never would have dreamed of.

A handful of local churches that had some connection to my family or Pastor Brooks contacted me to see if I would be willing to share my story at one of their church services. Every invitation was met with my eager anticipation. Keep in mind I was still smoking cigarettes heavily and I still had a foul mouth. In fact, before every service I spoke at, my friend Jeff would pray with me either in the car before going in or behind the platform what we called the "swear prayer." Swearing was my native language; we would pray for God to help me not swear while speaking in front of everyone. We also prayed that God would help me stop swearing altogether, but we thought the immediate situation of getting through a church service was a good place to start.

Telling what Jesus did for me never got old. It seemed like the tears would flow uncontrollably every time I talked about seeing Him. Some pastors and spiritually mature people told me that God had anointed me while sharing this story. I didn't know what anointed meant, but I did know that every time I shared my story I experienced such an overwhelming sense of His Spirit come over me that it felt as though His power was surging like a waterfall through my lips as I spoke. It didn't matter what it felt like (although it felt great). What mattered was I was seeing lives change right before my very eyes. It was amazing watching some of the people fall on their knees before God professing Him to be Lord. And they weren't the only ones changing. God was changing me daily. Like being in a raft careening down the wild rapids of a river, things were moving quickly in my life. There was purpose. There was life. The more people I saw come to Christ the more I wanted to see even more come to Christ. This became my new purpose and I wasn't going to let anything get in my way.

CHAPTER FIFTEEN
Conclusion

Never say never. On December 10, 1989 I smoked my last cigarette. And before that, immediately following the night of sharing my story at the evening service, church became my second home. Not only did I start attending church regularly, I volunteered 40 hours a week serving in every way from cleaning bathrooms to answering phones and assisting in a variety of other ways.

As it turned out Erin wasn't the girl for me after all. Six months after I shared my story at church, my dad loaned the tape recording of my story from that Sunday night to a young employee of his at Boeing by the name of Kim Sutton. After listening to the tape, Kim, full of curiosity, asked if I would be willing to meet with her so she could ask me some questions about my experience.

We met the following week at Denny's restaurant and we talked about life, God and eternity. She wanted to meet again the next night. On our fourth night in a row, meeting at Denny's, Kim gave her life to Jesus, and a couple years later she gave her hand to me in marriage on August 1, 1992.

The Bible says that in all things God works for the good of those who love Him and are called according to His purposes (Romans 8:28). In my most confusing times God was working out His plan even down to the detail of who I was to marry and how I was going to meet her. I cannot imagine myself with anyone else. God hand-picked Kim for me. We have been married nearly 20 years now and have two incredible teenagers (Brady & Heather). Together we have made it our goal to love God and to make His love known to others. We try to love those we come in contact with in such a way, that the message about Jesus is attractive to them. Through that attraction we pray they will come to a realization of God's love, forgiveness and power to heal.

I began to meet with Pastor Dennis Sawyer (the new Senior Pastor of CBSR at the time) weekly. He mentored me in my walk with Christ and was the reason I began pastoring. Under his tutelage, along with Pastor Brooks, they prepared me for what has now resulted in over 21 years of pastoring full time.

Pastor Sawyer hired me for the Youth Director position in 1990 at the age of 19. I worked full time on the CBSR staff for 11 years before they sent me, my family and 73 others to plant a new church in Kent, WA, in 2001. The name of the church is Riverview Community Church. We had our first service on Easter morning of 2001. Since then we have seen a great number of people come to a saving knowledge of Jesus Christ and surrender their lives to Him. It has been quite an experience to say the least. In my times of reflection, though, I have never forgotten where I came from and what led me to where I am today.

Before typing the last period to end this story I want to make something clear. I was not saved by having

a vision of Jesus in the woods. I was saved by what
He did for me over 2000 years ago on a cross. Jesus
came to earth to take our sin upon Himself so we
would be free from the punishment that sin incurs.
Being nailed to a cross, He paid the ultimate price
for your sins and mine. He did this so we could be
free from our debt that sin accumulated in our lives.
There is no greater thing He could ever do for you
than that. He may never appear to you in a vision or
speak an audible word to you. He may never walk
on water toward you or miraculously heal your body.
But what Jesus has done for me He has done for you.
We all have the same story. It's His story. We are all
lost until we are found. It is not a matter of what you
see, but what you believe. There were people who
saw Jesus with their own eyes; walked with Him,
listened to His stories and witnessed miracles and
some of them still died in their sin. The Bible says
we live by faith, not by sight (2 Corinthians 5:7). My
life has not been determined by something I saw, even
Jesus. It has been determined by God's grace and
my response to His grace. There are some who have
said, "Well, I would believe too if I saw Jesus" or

"It's easy for you to believe, you had that experience in the woods." The goodness of any experience is measured only by the nearness it brings you to truth and the results of embracing and applying that truth. It doesn't matter what kind of vision or experience you have. If Jesus is not your focus, you will never find the entrance to heaven. Apart from Holy Scripture my experience would have no eternal effect. Every miracle Jesus ever did and every appearance He ever made was for the purpose of clearly declaring who He is and what He did for mankind. He is the Savior of the world. There is no one like Him. In His own words He declares that He is the way, and the truth and the life and that no one can come to the Father except through Him (John 14:6). This is so vital to understand. Your destiny, not only on this earth but for eternity, depends upon your agreement with Jesus' teaching and acceptance of who He is and what He has done for you.

This might seem narrow minded. That's because it is. And that's a good thing. God has made our way to heaven easy. It is not a number of many paths that

end up at heaven's gate. It is one way, one person—
Jesus, and that is the truth. This was proved by the
resurrection of Jesus Christ. That was the greatest
act of God. It was and is His stamp of approval on
Jesus' teachings, life and final righteous act of dying
on the cross as the payment for man's sin.

I encourage you to read the Bible verses I have listed
in Appendix A at the back of this book as they will
help you better understand what I am saying.

I haven't been back on Bald Mountain for quite a
few hunting seasons and I haven't had a vision like
that one since. But I will say from that day on it
hasn't mattered whether I'm on the mountain tops or
in the valleys; Jesus Christ has been with me every
step of the way. He has never left me. And, frankly, I
haven't left Him either. My life has not been perfect.
Since my experience in 1989 I have had to overcome
a variety of obstacles. I have learned that life will
never be without its problems; but, our problems
don't need to leave us feeling lifeless.

If you feel like you are wandering aimlessly through life with no purpose or hope, with that sinking feeling of being lost, don't give up. Jesus is alive and He is near you, well aware of everything you are going through. Our human nature often compels us to run from the things or people we need the most. Please don't waste time running after the wrong things to fill the voids in your life. Run *to* Jesus not from Him. My prayer for you is that you would take Jesus at His word and put your trust in Him completely. And, by doing so discover, as I have, what life is really all about and see each day as a gift from God that needs to be lived out to the fullest until the day He welcomes us home to heaven.

If God has used my story and these Bible verses to stir up faith in you, then I want to encourage you to step out in that faith right now and say a simple prayer to God. There isn't a specific prayer you have to pray or some religious hoop you have to jump through. But just as with any relationship, growing close to God takes communication. Many people are afraid to pray because they have never done it

before and don't know what to say or how to say
it. Talk to God from your heart. What is on your
heart? Do you believe Jesus is the Son of God and
He died on the cross for your sins only to be raised
again on the third day? Tell Him you believe that.
Are you sorry for the sins you have committed in
your life and you want God to cleanse you from all
of them? Say that to Him. Do you want God to fill
you with His Spirit and empower you to live your life
for Him, impacting others along the way? Ask Him
for that. Go ahead and put this book down right now
and say those things to God if you really mean it. If
we confess our sins to Him He promises to forgive
us of our sins and cleanse us from every bad choice
we have made and the guilt that goes along with it.
You watch, God's Spirit will come into you and give
you a brand new life. And, one day, when it is your
turn to go to heaven, you will see Jesus face to face
and with a smile you will hear Him say "Welcome
Home."

Appendix – A
Bible Verses

All of the following Scriptures have been taken from
the NIV version of the Bible

Psalm 55:16 – But I call to God, and the Lord saves me.

Psalm 120:1 – I call on the Lord in my distress, and he answers me.

Psalm 145:18-19 – The Lord is near to all who call on him, to all who call on him in truth. He fulfills the desires of those who fear him; he hears their cry and saves them.

Luke 1:37 – …nothing is impossible with God.

John 3:16-18 – "For God so loved the world that he gave his one and only Son, that whoever believes in him shall not perish but have eternal life. For God did not send his Son into the world to condemn the world, but to save the world through him. Whoever believes in him is not condemned, but whoever does not believe stands condemned already because he has not believed in the name of God's one and only Son."

John 6:47 – I tell you the truth, he who believes has everlasting life.

Acts 2:38-39 – ... "Repent and be baptized, every one of you, in the name of Jesus Christ for the forgiveness of your sins. And you will receive the gift of the Holy Spirit. The promise is for you and your children and for all who are far off – for all whom the Lord our God will call."

Acts 16:31 – ... "Believe in the Lord Jesus, and you will be saved – you and your household."

Romans 3:23 – …all have sinned and fall short of the glory of God…

Romans 6:23 – For the wages of sin is death, but the gift of God is eternal life in Christ Jesus our Lord.

Romans 10:9-13 – …If you confess with your mouth, "Jesus is Lord," and believe in your heart that God raised him from the dead, you will be saved. For it is with your heart that you believe and are justified, and it is with your mouth that you confess and are saved. As the Scripture says, "Anyone who trusts in him will never be put to shame."…for, "Everyone who calls on the name of the Lord will be saved."

2 Corinthians 5:17 – Therefore, if anyone is in Christ, he is a new creation; the old has gone, the new has come.

Ephesians 2:8-10 – For it is by grace you have been saved, through faith – and this not from yourselves, it is the gift of God – not by works, so that no one can boast. For we are God's workmanship, created in Christ Jesus to do good works, which God prepared in advance for us to do.

Philippians 4:13 – I can do everything through him who gives me strength.

1 John 1:9 – If we confess our sins, he is faithful and just and will forgive us our sins and purify us from all unrighteousness.

Revelation 21:4 – He will wipe every tear from their eyes. There will be no more death or mourning or crying or pain, for the old order of things has passed away.

Appendix – B
Getting Help

Getting help with your depression is important. If you are suffering from depression make sure you get help. Don't hold this in.

As you put your trust in the Lord, your deliverance may come through some immediate awesome experience. But, for most, God often chooses to heal through a process that may seem less extravagant. There will be a number of decisions you are going to have to make to help bring about the healing of your mind and emotions. For example, reaching out to a friend, talking with a pastor or getting professional help should be one of the first things you consider doing.

Many things can be linked to depression. Your depression can be linked to a pattern of negative thoughts, low self-esteem, your diet, lack of exercise, past experiences not properly dealt with, your spiritual condition etc. All of these aspects of your life are interwoven together and when one is not doing good then it will start affecting the others as well.

Below are some websites and a toll-free number available for your help in overcoming depression and suicidal tendencies. I encourage you to check them out and to be proactive in doing what you can to really start enjoying the life God has given you.

National Institute of Mental Health
www.nimh.nih.gov

Mental Health America
www.mentalhealthamerica.net

National Suicide Prevention Lifeline
1-800-273-TALK (8255)

48370275R00057

Made in the USA
Charleston, SC
29 October 2015